MAXX CROSBY:

FROM SMALL TOWN TO NFL

SUPERSTAR

DORA N COUNTS

MAXX CROSBY

MAXX CROSBY

Disclaimer

The following book is for entertainment and informational purposes only. The information presented is without contract or any type of guarantee assurance. While every caution has been taken to provide accurate and current information, it is solely the reader's responsibility to check all information contained in this article before relying upon it. Neither the author nor the publisher can be held accountable for any errors or omissions. Under no circumstances will any legal responsibility or blame be held against the author or publisher for any reparation, damages, or monetary loss due to the information presented, either directly or indirectly. This book is not intended as legal or medical advice. If any such specialized advice is needed, seek a qualified individual for help.

Trademarks are used without permission. Use of the trademark is not authorized by, associated with, or sponsored by the trademark owners. All trademarks and brands used within this book are used with no intent to infringe on the trademark owners and are only used for clarifying purposes.

This book is not sponsored by or affiliated with American football,or anyone involved with them.

MAXX CROSBY

TABLE OF CONTENTS

INTRODUCTION

Maxx Crosby's journey from a small town to becoming one of the most feared defensive players in the NFL is nothing short of inspiring. Imagine growing up in a small town, dreaming of playing in the big leagues, and then one day, actually making it to the NFL! That's exactly what happened to Maxx Crosby. His story shows that with hard work, determination, and a belief in yourself, anything is possible — even reaching the highest levels of professional football. And the best part? His story isn't just about football; it's about pushing past challenges, staying focused, and never giving up, even when the odds seem stacked against you.

MAXX CROSBY

Maxx Crosby was born on August 22, 1997, in a small town in Michigan called Colleyville. From a young age, he showed a passion for sports, but football quickly became his favorite. Maxx loved the feeling of running onto the field, tackling opponents, and working together with his teammates. But it wasn't all easy for him. Maxx wasn't always the biggest or strongest player, and he faced many obstacles on his path to success. At times, it seemed like his dream of playing in the NFL might never come true. But Maxx never gave up.

When he was younger, Maxx played football just for the fun of it. But as he got older, he realized that he had the potential to go far. In high school, he worked harder than ever before, practicing every day and constantly trying to improve. Maxx knew that if he wanted to be great, he had to put in the effort, both on and off the field. He started paying attention to his diet, training harder, and studying the game to learn more about the strategies that would help him succeed.

Maxx Crosby didn't have the easiest path to the NFL. After finishing high school, he went to Eastern Michigan University, where he played college football. Eastern Michigan wasn't one of the big, famous schools like Alabama or Ohio State, where many NFL stars come from, but that didn't stop Maxx. He used his time there to prove himself and show that he could compete with the best players in the country. At Eastern Michigan, Maxx became known for his relentless work ethic and his ability to make big plays when his team needed him the most.

In 2019, Maxx's dream came true when he was drafted into the NFL by the Oakland Raiders (now the Las Vegas Raiders). For Maxx, this was a huge moment — all the years of hard work, dedication, and sacrifice had finally paid off. But even though he made it to the NFL, Maxx knew his journey was just beginning. He was determined to show that he belonged in the league and could become one of the best defensive players out there.

During his rookie season, Maxx quickly made a name for himself by constantly pressuring quarterbacks and making incredible plays. He didn't just settle for being on the team — he wanted to be a leader and help the Raiders win games. His passion and intensity on the field earned him respect from teammates, coaches, and fans alike.

What makes Maxx Crosby's story so special is that it shows how important it is to never give up on your dreams. Maxx wasn't always the biggest, fastest, or most talented player on the field, but he made up for it with heart, determination, and a willingness to outwork everyone around him. His story teaches us that success isn't just about talent — it's about perseverance, focus, and always believing in yourself.

In this book, we'll take a closer look at Maxx's incredible journey, from his early days in Colleyville to his rise as an NFL superstar. You'll

MAXX CROSBY

learn about the challenges he faced, the lessons
he learned, and the unforgettable moments that
have shaped his career. Maxx Crosby's story is
proof that no matter where you start, with
enough hard work and dedication, you can
achieve greatness.

CHAPTER 1: A SMALL TOWN DREAM

Maxx Crosby was born in a small town called Colleyville, Texas, where life was simple, but big dreams were always possible. Growing up, Maxx was just like many other kids in his town. He loved to play outside, hang out with his friends, and most of all, he loved sports. Whether it was running around in the yard or tossing a football with his friends, Maxx always seemed to be on the move. He was full of energy and determination, even at a young age.

As a young boy, Maxx didn't always think he would become a famous football player. In fact, there were times when he wasn't sure what he wanted to do when he grew up. But one thing was for sure—he had a strong love for sports. His parents always supported him, whether he was playing soccer, basketball, or football. They encouraged him to try different things and discover what he truly loved.

In his small town, football was a big deal. On Friday nights, the whole town would come together to watch the local high school football team play. The lights of the stadium would shine bright, and the crowd would cheer for their team. Watching these games sparked something inside Maxx. He admired the players and dreamed of one day playing under those same bright lights. He wanted to be part of something bigger than himself.

MAXX CROSBY

Maxx was always tall for his age, and his size made him stand out in sports. When he finally decided to give football a try, he knew it was the right choice. The first time he put on a helmet and pads, it felt like he had found his place. He was only in elementary school, but he already knew that football was special. Maxx practiced hard and gave his best effort every time he stepped onto the field. He wasn't the best player at first, but he had heart, and that's what made him stand out.

As Maxx grew older, he realized that his dream of playing football wasn't just about having fun. It was about pushing himself to be better every day. His dream was getting bigger and bigger, and Maxx knew that if he worked hard enough, he could turn his small-town dream into something amazing.

But it wasn't always easy. There were times when Maxx faced challenges and doubted himself. Sometimes, he wondered if he was good enough to play at a high level. But whenever he felt unsure, he remembered the Friday night games, the cheers of the crowd, and the way football made him feel alive. That's what kept him going.

Maxx's dream wasn't just about playing football; it was about proving to himself and to others that no matter where you come from, you can achieve big things if you work hard and never give up. He knew that dreams take time and effort, and he was willing to put in both.

MAXX CROSBY

In his small town of Colleyville, Maxx wasn't just a kid with a dream. He was a kid with determination, and that determination would soon take him far beyond the Friday night lights of his hometown. The journey was just beginning, and Maxx Crosby was ready to chase his dream, no matter what challenges came his way.

As he continued to grow and improve, Maxx's small-town dream of playing football would soon become a reality, one that would take him from the fields of Colleyville to the grand stages of the NFL. And it all started with a dream in a small town, a dream that Maxx never stopped believing in.

CHAPTER 2: DISCOVERING FOOTBALL

Maxx Crosby wasn't always sure that football would be his sport. Like many kids growing up in Colleyville, Texas, he enjoyed playing all kinds of sports. Whether it was running down the basketball court or kicking a soccer ball, Maxx loved being active. But football? That came a little later.

Maxx first discovered football when he was around eight years old. At first, it was just another game to play with his friends. They'd toss the football around in the backyard or during recess at school. Maxx was tall and fast for his age, which made him a natural at many sports, but when he picked up a football,

something clicked. He liked the way the ball felt
in his hands, the excitement of running down the
field, and the challenge of trying to outsmart
the other team.

Even though Maxx enjoyed playing football with
his friends, he wasn't sure if he was ready to
join an actual team. Football was tough, and the
idea of wearing all that gear—helmets, pads, and
cleats—seemed a little intimidating at first. But
when one of his friends asked if he wanted to
join the local football league, Maxx decided to
give it a try. After all, how would he know if he
liked it unless he tried?

Maxx's parents were supportive, as always. They
encouraged him to try new things and to follow
his interests. So, with their help, Maxx signed up

for his first football team. The first practice was exciting but nerve-wracking. Maxx put on his helmet and pads for the first time and looked around at the other kids on the field. Some of them had been playing football for a couple of years, while others, like Maxx, were just starting out.

At first, the practices were tough. Maxx had to learn all the rules of the game, and there were a lot of them! He had to figure out where to run, how to tackle, and when to pass the ball. Sometimes it felt overwhelming, but Maxx never gave up. He listened closely to his coaches and worked hard at every practice. He might not have been the best player on the team, but he was determined to get better.

MAXX CROSBY

One of the things Maxx loved most about football was teamwork. On the field, it wasn't just about what one person could do; it was about how the whole team worked together. Maxx liked that feeling of being part of something bigger, where every player had a role and everyone had to work together to win. It wasn't just about scoring touchdowns; it was about supporting his teammates, making good passes, and helping everyone play their best.

As the season went on, Maxx started to feel more confident. He learned how to move with the ball, how to block the other team, and how to find the best moments to make a play. The more he practiced, the more he realized that football wasn't just a fun game—it was something he was really good at.

MAXX CROSBY

Maxx's coaches noticed his hard work, too. Even though he was new to the sport, he was improving every day. They saw his dedication and the way he never gave up, even when things got tough. Maxx was learning that football wasn't just about skill; it was also about heart, and Maxx had plenty of that.

By the end of his first season, Maxx knew that football was the sport for him. He loved everything about it—the excitement of the games, the friendships he made with his teammates, and the thrill of improving every day. Football had become more than just a game; it was a passion. And even though Maxx was still young, he started to dream big. He knew that if he kept working hard, there was no limit to what he could achieve in the world of football.

Little did he know, his journey in football was only beginning, and much bigger challenges and opportunities were waiting just around the corner. Maxx Crosby had discovered his love for football, and now, he was ready to see where it would take him.

CHAPTER 3: HIGH SCHOOL CHALLENGES

When Maxx Crosby started high school, things began to change. High school football was much more competitive than anything he had experienced before. The players were bigger, stronger, and faster, and the games were more intense. Maxx knew he had to work harder than ever if he wanted to stand out.

At first, it wasn't easy. Maxx had to balance schoolwork with football practice, and sometimes it felt like there wasn't enough time in the day. High school classes were tougher, with more homework and tests, and football practice became even more demanding. His coaches expected a lot from the team, and Maxx often found himself feeling exhausted after long practices. But Maxx wasn't the type to give up. He loved football too much.

Maxx faced some tough moments early on. He wasn't always the biggest player on the field, and sometimes it felt like other players were stronger or faster than him. During his first year on the high school football team, Maxx didn't always get a lot of playing time. It was frustrating to sit on the sidelines and watch as others got the chance to show their skills. He wanted to prove that he had what it took to be a key player, but he knew he had to be patient.

Instead of feeling discouraged, Maxx used this time to learn. He paid close attention to the older, more experienced players on the team. He watched how they played, how they moved on the field, and how they handled challenges. Maxx also listened carefully to his coaches' advice. They told him that football wasn't just about physical strength; it was about understanding the game and working as a team.

During his sophomore year, Maxx started to see some changes. He had grown stronger and more confident, and he was determined to prove himself. He spent extra hours at the gym, working on his strength and conditioning. Maxx knew that if he wanted to compete with the best players, he needed to be in top shape. He also focused on improving his skills—practicing his tackles, his footwork, and his overall understanding of the game.

MAXX CROSBY

All the hard work began to pay off. By his junior
year, Maxx had earned a starting spot on the
team. It wasn't easy, but Maxx had shown his
coaches and teammates that he was ready for
the challenge. He was playing against some of
the best high school teams in the area, and the
competition was fierce. Maxx learned that every
game was a battle, and he had to give his best
effort every time he stepped onto the field.

But even as Maxx improved, high school football
brought its own set of challenges. Sometimes,
Maxx would get knocked down during a game, or
his team would lose a tough match. There were
days when the pressure felt overwhelming, and
Maxx wondered if he was good enough to keep
going. But every time he faced a setback, Maxx

reminded himself why he started playing football in the first place: because he loved the game.

Maxx's family and friends were always there to support him. His parents encouraged him to keep going, reminding him that every challenge was a chance to grow stronger. His coaches believed in him, too, pushing him to improve with every practice and every game. And Maxx's teammates became like a second family, helping each other through tough times and celebrating each other's victories.

By the time Maxx was a senior, he had become one of the leaders of his team. He wasn't just playing football—he was helping his teammates grow and succeed, too. High school football had taught him a lot about hard work, perseverance, and teamwork. He had faced challenges, but he had overcome them through determination and passion.

Maxx knew that his journey in football was far from over. The next step would be even bigger—college football. But after everything he had learned in high school, Maxx was ready for whatever came next. He had grown into a strong, confident player, and he was excited to chase his dreams on an even bigger stage.

CHAPTER 4: COLLEGE DAYS AT EASTERN MICHIGAN

After a successful high school football career, Maxx Crosby was ready for the next big step: college football. He earned a spot on the team at Eastern Michigan University (EMU), a school with a strong football program. Maxx was excited but also a bit nervous. College football was a whole new level, with faster players, tougher competition, and more intense practices.

When Maxx first arrived at Eastern Michigan, he was one of many new players trying to make their mark. The team was full of talented athletes from all over the country, and Maxx knew that he had to work harder than ever to stand out. But Maxx was up for the challenge. He

MAXX CROSBY

had always been determined, and now that he had made it to college football, he wasn't going to let anything stop him.

College football wasn't just about playing on Saturdays—it was about preparing every day. Maxx quickly learned that being a college athlete meant long days of training, studying game plans, and balancing schoolwork with practice. He had to wake up early for weightlifting sessions, followed by hours of practice on the field. After that, there were team meetings, video reviews, and, of course, time in the classroom. It wasn't easy, but Maxx knew that this was all part of becoming a better player.

At first, Maxx didn't get a lot of playing time. Like in high school, he had to prove himself all over again. But Maxx was patient. He spent his freshman year working hard, learning from the older players, and improving his skills. He paid attention to the details—how to read the game, where to position himself, and how to use his strength to outplay his opponents.

By his sophomore year, Maxx's dedication started to pay off. He was getting more playing time and making a name for himself as a talented defensive end. His speed and power on the field were catching the attention of his coaches and teammates. Maxx had a knack for getting to the quarterback and making big plays. He became known for his aggressive style of play, always pushing himself to go the extra mile to help his team.

MAXX CROSBY

One of the things that set Maxx apart was his relentless work ethic. He didn't just rely on his natural talent—he spent extra hours in the gym, watching game film, and working with his coaches to improve. Maxx knew that if he wanted to succeed at the college level, he had to put in the work every day. And that's exactly what he did.

As Maxx continued to rise through the ranks, he faced some tough challenges, too. College football was demanding, both physically and mentally. There were times when Maxx felt the pressure of balancing his academic responsibilities with the intense demands of football. But he never gave up. Maxx leaned on his family, his coaches, and his teammates for support, and he pushed through the tough times with grit and determination.

MAXX CROSBY

By the time Maxx was a junior, he had established himself as one of Eastern Michigan's best players. He was a leader on the field, helping his team win crucial games and setting an example for younger players. Maxx's hard work and dedication had paid off, and he was starting to attract attention from scouts who recognized his potential to play at the professional level.

Maxx's college career wasn't just about football, though. He also learned important life lessons during his time at Eastern Michigan. He learned how to stay focused under pressure, how to be a team player, and how to push himself to achieve his goals. Maxx's time in college helped him grow, both as a football player and as a person.

MAXX CROSBY

As Maxx prepared for his senior year, he knew that his dreams of playing in the NFL were within reach. But first, he had to finish what he started at Eastern Michigan. Maxx was ready to give his all, knowing that every game, every practice, and every challenge had brought him one step closer to achieving his ultimate goal: becoming an NFL player.

Maxx's college days were filled with hard work, growth, and unforgettable moments. He had faced challenges, but with determination and passion, he had overcome them. Now, as he looked ahead to the future, Maxx knew that his journey was far from over. The NFL was waiting, and Maxx was ready to take the next big step in his football career.

CHAPTER 5: GETTING DRAFTED: THE NFL CALL

For Maxx Crosby, the dream of playing in the NFL was always in his heart, but getting drafted was a huge moment in his life. After years of hard work in high school and college football, it was finally time to see if his name would be called by one of the NFL teams. This process is known as the NFL Draft, where professional teams pick new players from college football to join their rosters.

The NFL Draft is a big deal. Players, coaches, and fans all watch as the best football players in the country wait to hear their names called. Maxx was excited but also nervous. Would a team pick him? Would he get the chance to prove himself in the NFL, the biggest stage for football?

Maxx knew the draft process wasn't easy. Scouts and coaches from NFL teams watch hours of game footage and hold interviews to see which players they want. They look at everything—from how well a player performs on the field to how they handle pressure. Maxx had worked so hard at Eastern Michigan, and now he hoped that his performance would be enough to impress the NFL teams.

When the draft finally came, Maxx waited anxiously with his family. It was a long process, spread out over several days. The first round of the draft is where the top players get picked, and while Maxx knew he was a talented player, he didn't expect to go in the first round. That didn't discourage him, though. Maxx stayed patient, knowing that he just needed one team to believe in him.

As the rounds went by, Maxx's excitement grew. He knew his time was coming. Then, in the fourth round, Maxx got the news he had been dreaming of: the Oakland Raiders wanted him on their team! When the call came in, Maxx couldn't believe it—he was officially drafted into the NFL. His dream had come true!

Maxx's family was overjoyed, and so was he. All those years of hard work had paid off, and now he had the chance to play at the highest level of football. Getting drafted was just the beginning, though. Maxx knew he would need to work even harder in the NFL. The competition would be tougher, and the expectations would be higher. But Maxx was ready for the challenge.

Being drafted into the NFL is a special moment for any player, but for Maxx, it was also a moment of gratitude. He thanked his family, his coaches, and everyone who had helped him along the way. Maxx had always been determined, but he knew he hadn't done it alone. His journey to the NFL was made possible by the support and encouragement of the people around him.

Joining the Oakland Raiders was a huge step, but Maxx didn't let the excitement distract him from his goals. He knew he had to prove himself all over again. The NFL was a whole new level, and Maxx was ready to show that he belonged there. He packed his bags, said goodbye to his college days, and headed off to start the next chapter of his football career.

When Maxx arrived at the Raiders' training camp, he was greeted by new coaches and teammates. It was a bit overwhelming at first—everything felt bigger, faster, and more intense. But Maxx was used to challenges, and he approached this one the same way he had always done: with hard work and determination.

The NFL Draft was an unforgettable moment in Maxx's life. It marked the beginning of his journey as a professional football player. While many people see getting drafted as the end of a long road, for Maxx, it was the start of something even bigger. He knew that his real work was just beginning. Now, it was time to take on the NFL, show his skills, and continue chasing his dream of becoming one of the best players in the league.

Maxx's draft day was a day filled with excitement, joy, and pride. It was proof that dreams really do come true if you work hard and never give up. Maxx had made it to the NFL, and the sky was the limit!

CHAPTER 6: ROOKIE SEASON: PROVING HIMSELF

Maxx Crosby was officially an NFL player, drafted by the Oakland Raiders. The excitement of being drafted was amazing, but now the real challenge was just beginning. Maxx was about to face his rookie season in the NFL, where he would have to prove himself to his coaches, teammates, and fans.

Being a rookie means it's your first year playing as a professional, and everyone's watching to see how you'll perform. The NFL is the highest level of football in the world, and Maxx knew that playing in the NFL would be tougher than anything he had experienced before. The players were faster, stronger, and more skilled, but Maxx was ready to give it his all.

When Maxx arrived at the Raiders' training camp, he felt the energy and intensity. He was surrounded by experienced players who had been in the NFL for years. But instead of feeling nervous, Maxx felt inspired. He wanted to learn from them and improve every day. He knew that if he worked hard, he could earn his place on the team.

The coaches were also paying close attention to Maxx. They saw his potential, but they wanted to see if he could handle the pressure. Training camp was tough. Maxx spent hours on the field practicing, lifting weights in the gym, and studying the playbook. He had to be strong physically and mentally. Maxx pushed himself harder than ever before because he wanted to prove that he belonged in the NFL.

When the regular season started, Maxx was excited but also a little nervous. Would he get a chance to play in the games? Would he be able to show everyone what he could do? The first few games were a learning experience. Maxx watched and listened, soaking up advice from the veteran players. Then, when the opportunity came, Maxx took the field with determination.

In his rookie season, Maxx played as a defensive end, a position where the goal is to stop the opposing team's offense, especially by tackling the quarterback or preventing running plays. Maxx's job was to use his speed and strength to break through the offensive line and make big plays for his team.

And Maxx did just that! In one of his early games, he made an incredible play by sacking the opposing team's quarterback. A sack is when a defensive player tackles the quarterback behind the line of scrimmage, stopping the play and causing the other team to lose yards. It's a huge moment in any game, and Maxx's sack made everyone stand up and cheer.

Maxx's performance during his rookie season didn't go unnoticed. He continued to work hard, and by the end of the season, he had made several big plays, including more sacks and tackles. He was quickly becoming a key player on the Raiders' defense.

But Maxx didn't let the success go to his head. He knew that one good season didn't mean the hard work was over. Instead, it made him even more determined to improve. He wanted to become one of the best defensive players in the NFL, and that meant continuing to train and push himself.

One of the most important things Maxx learned during his rookie season was the value of teamwork. Football isn't a game where one player can win it all by themselves. Maxx had to work closely with his teammates, communicate on the field, and trust each other. Together, they could stop the other team and win games.

MAXX CROSBY

Maxx's rookie season was a huge success. He proved to everyone that he was more than just a college football star—he was a real NFL player with a bright future ahead of him. The fans loved his energy and determination, and his coaches were proud of how far he had come.

As Maxx's rookie season came to an end, he looked back on everything he had accomplished. It had been a year full of challenges, but also of victories. Maxx had proven himself in the NFL, and he was ready for whatever came next. He knew that this was only the beginning of a long and exciting journey in professional football.

CHAPTER 7: BECOMING A LEADER ON THE FIELD

As Maxx Crosby continued his journey in the NFL, his rookie season taught him a lot. He had learned how to handle the challenges and pressure of professional football, but there was still more to achieve. Now, it was time for Maxx to take on a new role: becoming a leader on the field.

Being a leader in football is more than just being good at playing the game. It means guiding and inspiring your teammates, helping them improve, and showing them how to work together as a team. Maxx knew that to be a great leader, he needed to lead by example. He wanted to make a

difference on the field and help his team
succeed.

During the offseason, Maxx worked hard to get
even better. He knew that if he wanted to be a
leader, he had to keep improving his skills. He
spent extra time in the gym, practiced his
techniques, and studied game footage to
understand how he could make better plays.
Maxx wanted to be the best defensive end he
could be, and he knew that required dedication
and effort.

When the new season started, Maxx was ready
to show his teammates that he was not only a
strong player but also a leader. On the field, he
focused on making big plays and setting a good
example. He gave his best effort in every game

and encouraged his teammates to do the same.
Maxx was always the first to arrive at practice
and the last to leave, showing his commitment
and hard work.

One of the most important ways Maxx showed
his leadership was through his communication.
Football is a team sport where players have to
work closely together. Maxx made sure to talk
with his teammates, discuss strategies, and help
them understand their roles. He used his
experience to guide the younger players, sharing
tips and advice that he had learned from his own
experiences.

Maxx also became known for his positive
attitude. Even when things didn't go as planned
or when the team faced tough challenges, Maxx

stayed upbeat and motivated. He knew that a positive attitude could boost the morale of the whole team. His energy and enthusiasm were contagious, and they helped keep everyone focused and determined.

One memorable moment that showed Maxx's leadership was during a crucial game where the team was falling behind. The players were feeling frustrated and unsure of themselves. Maxx gathered his teammates and gave an inspiring speech. He reminded them of their strengths, encouraged them to believe in each other, and urged them to keep fighting until the final whistle. Maxx's words and actions helped the team rally together, and they managed to turn the game around and win.

MAXX CROSBY

Off the field, Maxx continued to build strong
relationships with his teammates. He organized
team events and gatherings, creating
opportunities for everyone to bond and get to
know each other better. Building trust and
camaraderie among the players was an important
part of being a leader, and Maxx made sure to
foster a positive and supportive team
environment.

Maxx's leadership didn't go unnoticed. His
coaches and teammates respected him not only
for his skills but also for his ability to inspire
and lead. They admired his dedication, his
positive attitude, and his willingness to help
others. Maxx had become a key figure in the
team, someone who others looked up to and
relied on.

MAXX CROSBY

As the season continued, Maxx's role as a leader grew stronger. He continued to work hard, lead by example, and support his teammates. Maxx knew that being a leader was a responsibility, but he embraced it with enthusiasm and determination. He wanted to help his team achieve their goals and make a positive impact both on and off the field.

By becoming a leader, Maxx Crosby showed that being successful in football isn't just about being a great player. It's also about inspiring others, working together, and making a difference in the team. Maxx's journey from a rookie to a leader was a testament to his hard work, dedication, and love for the game.

CHAPTER 8: BIG PLAYS AND MEMORABLE MOMENTS

Maxx Crosby's journey in the NFL was filled with exciting games and unforgettable moments. As he grew more experienced, he started making big plays that fans and teammates would remember for years. Let's dive into some of the most memorable moments of Maxx's career!

One of the most thrilling parts of being a football player is making a big play that helps your team win. Maxx Crosby had many chances to shine on the field, and he took every opportunity to show just how talented he was. Let's look at a few of his standout plays.

MAXX CROSBY

One memorable game was against a team that was known for its strong offense. Maxx and his team were up against some tough competition. The game was close, and every play counted. In the fourth quarter, with just minutes left on the clock, the opposing team was driving towards the end zone. The tension was high, and everyone in the stadium was on the edge of their seats.

Maxx saw his chance to make a difference. With incredible speed and determination, he raced past the offensive line and reached the quarterback just as he was about to throw the ball. Maxx leaped into the air and made a huge tackle, knocking the quarterback to the ground. The crowd erupted in cheers, and Maxx's teammates celebrated with high-fives and hugs. That play stopped the opposing team's drive and helped secure the victory for Maxx's team. It was a play that fans would talk about for a long time!

Another exciting moment came when Maxx made a crucial sack during a game that was tied. The opposing team was trying to score a game-winning touchdown. Maxx knew this was a critical moment, so he put all his focus and energy into the play. As the quarterback dropped back to pass, Maxx broke through the line and tackled him before he could throw the ball. The sack pushed the opposing team back, making it harder for them to score. Maxx's big play helped his team stay in the game and eventually win.

MAXX CROSBY

Maxx also had some amazing interceptions, which are rare for a defensive end. One of these interceptions happened during a game where Maxx was determined to make an impact. The quarterback threw a pass, and Maxx managed to get his hands on the ball, catching it before it hit the ground. It was a surprising and exciting moment that showed off Maxx's quick reflexes and athleticism. The crowd cheered wildly as Maxx ran the ball back, gaining valuable yards for his team.

Besides these big plays, Maxx made sure to be a positive influence on his team. He often encouraged his teammates, celebrating their successes and helping them through tough times. During one game, Maxx noticed that a younger player was feeling nervous and was not

MAXX CROSBY

performing at his best. Maxx took the time to talk to him, offering advice and encouragement. The young player's confidence grew, and he ended up making some key plays that helped the team win. Maxx's leadership and support were just as important as his on-field performance.

Maxx's big plays and memorable moments were not only exciting but also inspiring. They showed how hard work, dedication, and a love for the game could lead to incredible achievements. Maxx's fans and teammates looked up to him, not just for his skill, but for his ability to make the game fun and exciting for everyone involved.

As Maxx continued his career, he knew that every game was a chance to create new memories and make more big plays. He remained focused, worked hard, and always gave his best effort. Each play he made added to his story and helped shape his legacy as a great football player.

Maxx Crosby's career was filled with thrilling moments and exciting plays that fans will remember for years to come. His journey showed that with passion and perseverance, anyone can achieve their dreams and create their own unforgettable moments.

CHAPTER 9: OVERCOMING SETBACKS AND STAYING STRONG

Even the most successful athletes face challenges and setbacks along their journey. Maxx Crosby's path to becoming a top NFL player was not always smooth. There were times when things didn't go as planned, but Maxx showed incredible strength and determination in overcoming these obstacles.

One of the biggest challenges Maxx faced was dealing with injuries. Injuries are a part of sports, and even the best players can get hurt. During one season, Maxx suffered a significant injury that kept him off the field for several games. It was a tough time for him, as he missed playing with his teammates and helping his team win. But Maxx didn't let this setback get him down. Instead, he focused on his recovery, working hard in physical therapy and staying positive.

While he was recovering, Maxx made sure to stay involved with his team. He attended meetings, cheered on his teammates from the sidelines, and offered support and advice. Even though he couldn't play, Maxx's presence and encouragement were important to his team. He knew that staying engaged and motivated was key to bouncing back stronger.

Maxx also faced challenges when he struggled with his performance. There were games where he didn't play as well as he wanted to, and he felt disappointed in himself. But Maxx didn't give up. Instead of letting these tough moments get to him, he used them as motivation to work harder. He practiced extra hours, studied game footage, and learned from his mistakes. Maxx knew that setbacks were a chance to grow and improve.

During one particularly difficult stretch, Maxx faced criticism from fans and media. Some people doubted his abilities and questioned his place on the team. This was a tough time for Maxx, as it can be hard to hear negative comments about something you care deeply about. However, Maxx chose to focus on his goals and the support from his family, friends, and teammates. He reminded himself why he loved playing football and used the criticism as fuel to prove himself even more.

Maxx's journey also included moments of self-doubt. Every athlete experiences times when they question their abilities or wonder if they can achieve their dreams. Maxx had these moments too, but he learned to stay strong and believe in himself. He set small goals and celebrated each achievement, no matter how big or small. By doing this, Maxx built his confidence and stayed on track towards his larger dreams.

One important lesson Maxx learned was the value of perseverance. Even when things got tough, he didn't give up. He understood that success is not just about winning games but also about handling the challenges that come along the way. Maxx's ability to stay focused and keep pushing forward, even during difficult times, was a key part of his success.

Maxx's story is a reminder that everyone faces challenges and setbacks, no matter how talented or successful they are. What matters most is how you handle these moments. Maxx showed that by staying strong, working hard, and believing in yourself, you can overcome obstacles and keep moving towards your goals.

Through his determination and resilience, Maxx Crosby became not just a great football player but also an inspiring example of how to face challenges with courage and positivity. His journey teaches us that setbacks are just part of the adventure, and with the right attitude,

you can turn them into opportunities for growth
and success.

CHAPTER 10: LOOKING AHEAD: MAXX CROSBY'S FUTURE

As Maxx Crosby looks towards the future, his journey is far from over. Even though he has already achieved so much, there are exciting new goals and dreams that lie ahead for him. Let's explore what Maxx might have in store for the coming years and how he plans to continue making a difference both on and off the field.

Maxx Crosby's success in the NFL has been impressive, but he's not one to rest on his laurels. He knows that to stay at the top of his game, he needs to keep working hard. Maxx sets new goals for himself every year, whether it's improving his skills, achieving more sacks, or helping his team win important games. He is always looking for ways to challenge himself and grow as a player. This drive for continuous improvement is a big part of what makes him stand out.

One of Maxx's biggest dreams is to win a Super Bowl. He has already proven himself as a talented player, but winning the championship is a special goal that many athletes aspire to. Maxx and his team are always working towards that big win. He knows that it takes dedication, teamwork, and a lot of hard work to reach the Super Bowl, and he is committed to giving it his all.

MAXX CROSBY

In addition to his football career, Maxx Crosby is also passionate about giving back to his community. He has been involved in various charitable activities and community events. Maxx understands the importance of using his platform to make a positive impact on others' lives. Whether it's supporting local youth programs, participating in charity events, or simply inspiring kids with his story, Maxx wants to make a difference both on and off the field.

Maxx is also focused on maintaining a healthy lifestyle and staying fit. He knows that being an athlete requires taking care of his body, so he follows a strict training and nutrition regimen. Maxx works closely with coaches and trainers to ensure that he stays in top shape. His commitment to staying healthy is crucial for his performance and long-term success in the NFL.

As he continues his career, Maxx Crosby will also be a role model for young athletes. He loves sharing his experiences and encouraging kids to pursue their dreams. Maxx's story shows that with hard work, dedication, and perseverance, you can achieve great things. He hopes to inspire the next generation of football players to follow their passions and never give up on their goals.

Looking further into the future, Maxx might also explore opportunities beyond football. Athletes often find new interests and ventures after their playing careers. Maxx could take on roles in sports media, coaching, or even entrepreneurship. Whatever path he chooses,

MAXX CROSBY

Maxx's determination and work ethic will likely lead him to success in whatever he decides to pursue.

Maxx Crosby's future is filled with possibilities. He has already accomplished so much, but he is excited about what's to come. His focus on continuous improvement, community involvement, and being a positive role model will help guide him as he navigates the next chapters of his life. Maxx's story is a testament to the power of dreaming big, working hard, and always looking ahead. With his passion and drive, there's no doubt that Maxx Crosby will continue to achieve great things and inspire others along the way.

CONCLUSION

As we close the pages of Maxx Crosby's journey, it's clear that his story is one of incredible hard work, dedication, and dreaming big. From a small town in Michigan to becoming a star in the NFL, Maxx Crosby's life shows us that with passion and perseverance, anything is possible.

Maxx's journey began in his hometown, where he first discovered his love for football. It wasn't always easy—he faced challenges and obstacles along the way, but he never gave up. Whether it was working hard in high school, pushing through tough college games, or proving himself as a rookie in the NFL, Maxx always kept his eyes on his dreams.

MAXX CROSBY

One of the most inspiring things about Maxx is his never-give-up attitude. He didn't let any setbacks stop him. Instead, he used them as opportunities to grow stronger and better. His story teaches us that even when things get tough, staying focused and working hard can help us overcome any challenge.

Maxx also shows us the importance of giving back. Even though he's a big NFL star now, he never forgets where he came from. He uses his success to help others, whether it's through community service, supporting youth programs, or simply being a positive role model. Maxx's generosity reminds us that we can all make a difference in our own way.

MAXX CROSBY

Looking ahead, Maxx Crosby's future is bright. He has big dreams and goals, and he continues to work hard to achieve them. Whether it's winning a Super Bowl, staying healthy, or inspiring young athletes, Maxx is dedicated to making the most of his career and life.

Maxx Crosby's story is more than just about football; it's about following your dreams, working hard, and being a good person. It shows us that with determination and a positive attitude, we can all reach for the stars, no matter where we start.

So, as you finish this book, remember Maxx's journey and let it inspire you to chase your own dreams. Whether you want to be a star athlete, a scientist, or an artist, Maxx Crosby's story proves that with passion, hard work, and a little bit of grit, you can achieve amazing things. Keep believing in yourself, keep working hard, and remember that every great journey starts with a dream.

FUN FACTS ABOUT MAXX CROSBY

Football Fanatic: Maxx Crosby has loved football since he was a little kid. He used to watch games with his family and dreamed of one day playing in the NFL.

College Star: Even though he went to a smaller college, Eastern Michigan University, Maxx Crosby made a big impact and caught the attention of NFL scouts with his amazing skills.

Rookie Success: In his very first NFL season, Maxx Crosby played so well that he was named to the NFL All-Rookie Team, which is a big honor for new players!

MAXX CROSBY

Nickname: Maxx Crosby's friends and teammates sometimes call him "Maxx Attack" because of his aggressive playing style on the field.

Hometown Hero: Maxx grew up in a small town in Michigan, and he often talks about how his hometown helped shape his work ethic and determination.

Charitable Spirit: Off the field, Maxx Crosby loves helping others. He is involved in charity work and often participates in events to support kids and families in need.

Fitness Fanatic: Maxx is known for his intense workouts. He spends hours training to stay in top shape, and he enjoys sharing fitness tips with his fans.

Family Support: Maxx's family has always been his biggest cheerleaders. They traveled with him to games and supported him through every step of his football career.

Favorite NFL Player: Growing up, Maxx looked up to NFL stars like Ray Lewis. He admired their passion and hard work, and he wanted to follow in their footsteps.

Dream Chaser: Maxx Crosby's story shows that even if you come from a small town, with hard work and determination, you can achieve big dreams, just like becoming an NFL superstar!

QUIZ!QUIZ!!QUIZ!!!

Where was Maxx Crosby born?

a) California

b) Texas

c) Michigan

d) New York

Answer: c) Michigan

2. What position does Maxx Crosby play in football?

a) Quarterback

b) Running Back

c) Defensive End

d) Wide Receiver

Answer: c) Defensive End

3. Which college did Maxx Crosby attend?

a) Michigan State

b) Eastern Michigan

c) Ohio State

d) Penn State

Answer: b) Eastern Michigan

4. In which year was Maxx Crosby drafted into the NFL?

a) 2016

b) 2018

c) 2019

d) 2020

Answer: c) 2019

MAXX CROSBY

5. What team did Maxx Crosby join when he entered the NFL?

a) New England Patriots

b) Los Angeles Rams

c) Las Vegas Raiders

d) Denver Broncos

Answer: c) Las Vegas Raiders

6. What is one of Maxx Crosby's favorite hobbies outside of football?

a) Painting

b) Playing video games

c) Cooking

d) Fishing

Answer: d) Fishing

MAXX CROSBY

7. How many sacks did Maxx Crosby have in his
rookie NFL season?

a) 10

b) 6

c) 12

d) 8

Answer: b) 10

8. What is Maxx Crosby known for on and off
the field?

a) Singing

b) His strong work ethic

c) Dancing

d) Playing guitar

Answer: b) His strong work ethic

MAXX CROSBY

9. Which high school did Maxx Crosby attend?

a) Notre Dame Prep

b) Farmington High

c) Rockford High

d) Lansing High

Answer: a) Notre Dame Prep

10. Maxx Crosby's success story shows that you can achieve your dreams by:

a) Always staying at home

b) Giving up easily

c) Working hard and never giving up

d) Waiting for opportunities to come

Answer: c) Working hard and never giving up

Made in the USA
Columbia, SC
21 October 2024

44808867R00046